I0762634

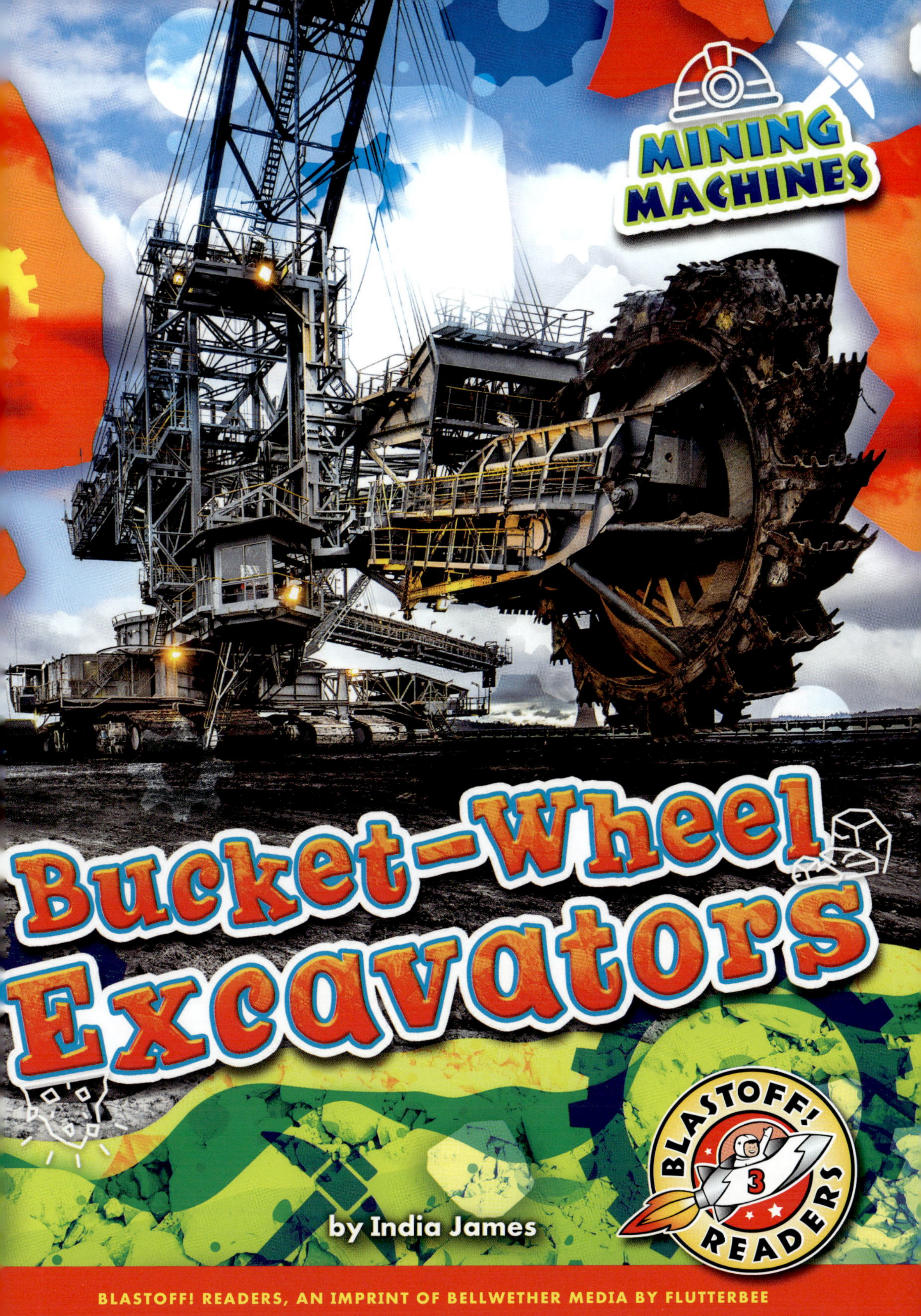

BLASTOFF! READERS, AN IMPRINT OF BELLWETHER MEDIA BY FLUTTERBEE

Blastoff! Readers are carefully developed by literacy experts to build reading stamina and move students toward fluency by combining standards-based content with developmentally appropriate text.

LEVELS

Level 1 provides the most support through repetition of high-frequency words, light text, predictable sentence patterns, and strong visual support.

Level 2 offers early readers a bit more challenge through varied sentences, increased text load, and text-supportive special features.

Level 3 advances early-fluent readers toward fluency through increased text load, less reliance on photos, advancing concepts, longer sentences, and more complex special features.

★ **Blastoff! Universe**

Reading Level

Blastoff! Beginners — Grade K

Grades 1–3

Grade 4

This edition first published in 2027 by Bellwether Media, Inc.

For information regarding permission, write to Bellwether Media, Inc., Attention: Permissions Department, 3500 American Blvd W, Suite 150, Bloomington, MN 55431.

Library of Congress Cataloging-in-Publication Data is available at www.loc.gov or upon request from the publisher.

ISBN: 9798898800697 (hardcover)
ISBN: 9798898801939 (ebook)

Editor: Kieran Downs   Designer: Jeffrey Kollock

Printed in the United States of America, North Mankato, MN.

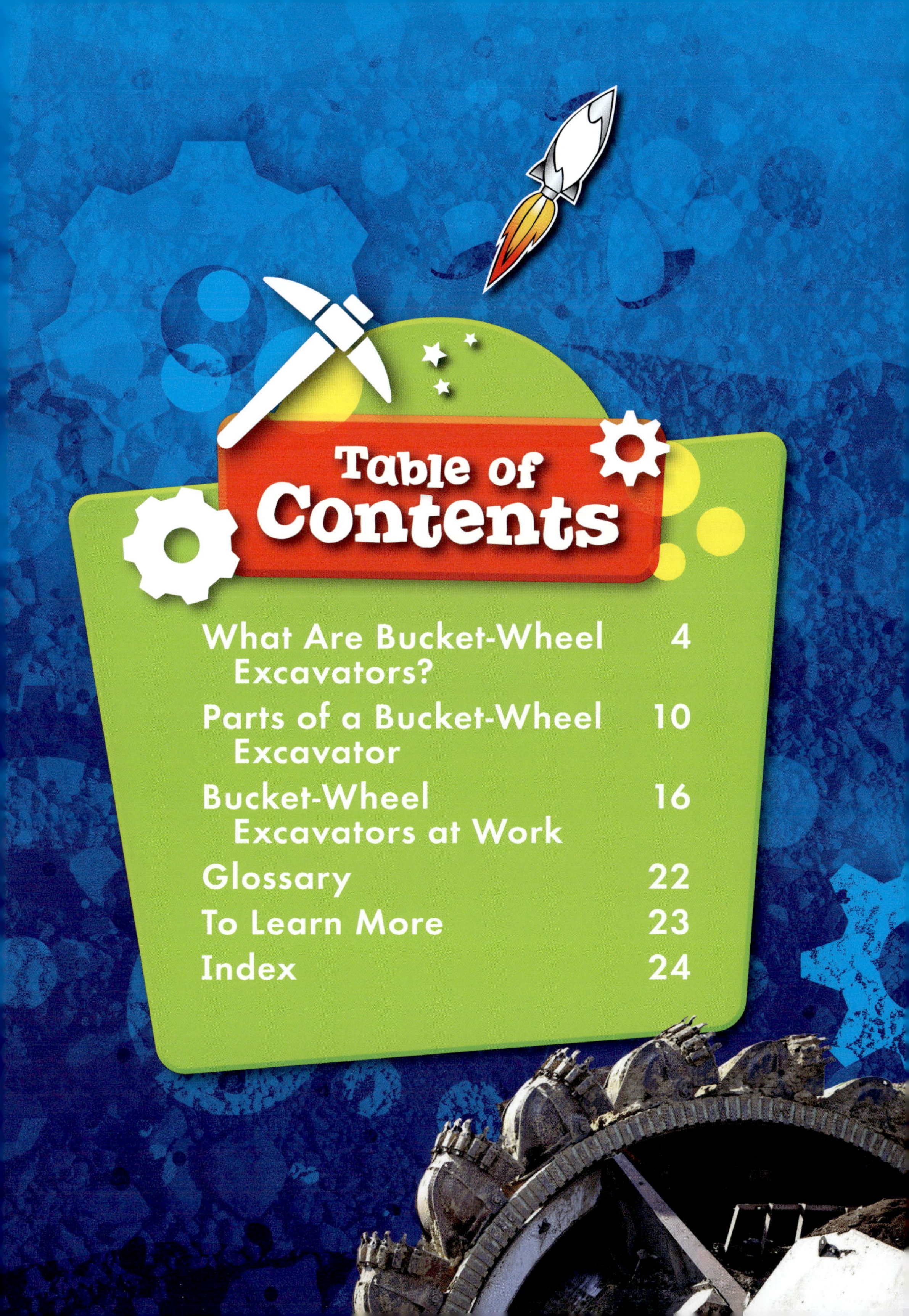

Table of Contents

What Are Bucket-Wheel Excavators?

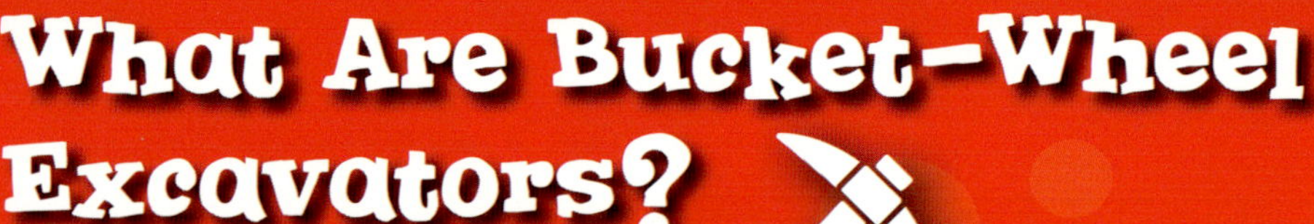

Bucket-wheel excavators are huge machines. They are used to cut through the ground.

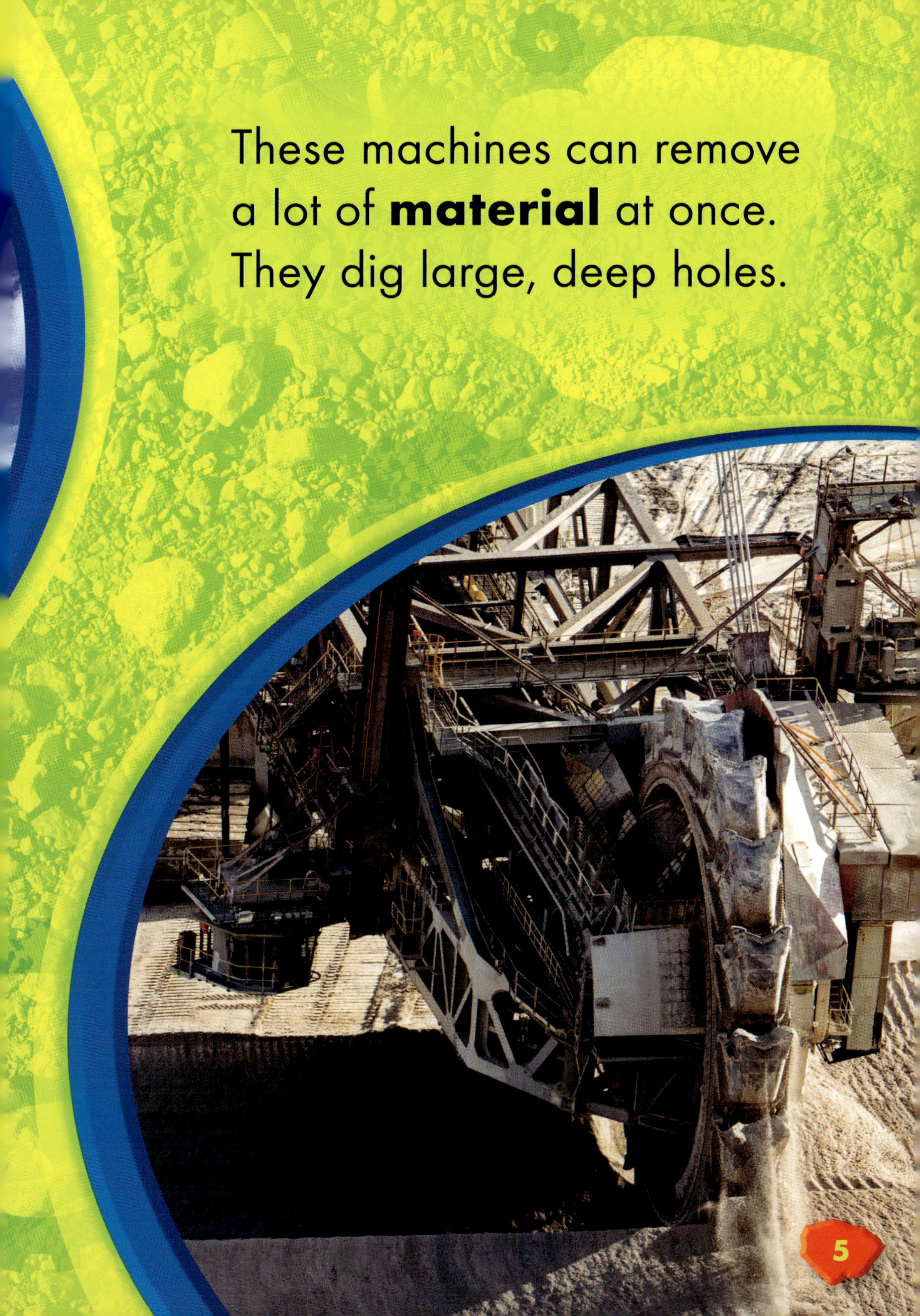

These machines can remove a lot of **material** at once. They dig large, deep holes.

There are different types of bucket-wheel excavators. **Compact** bucket-wheel excavators are smaller. Their frames are shaped like an L.

Giant bucket-wheel excavators are larger. Their frames are shaped like a C.

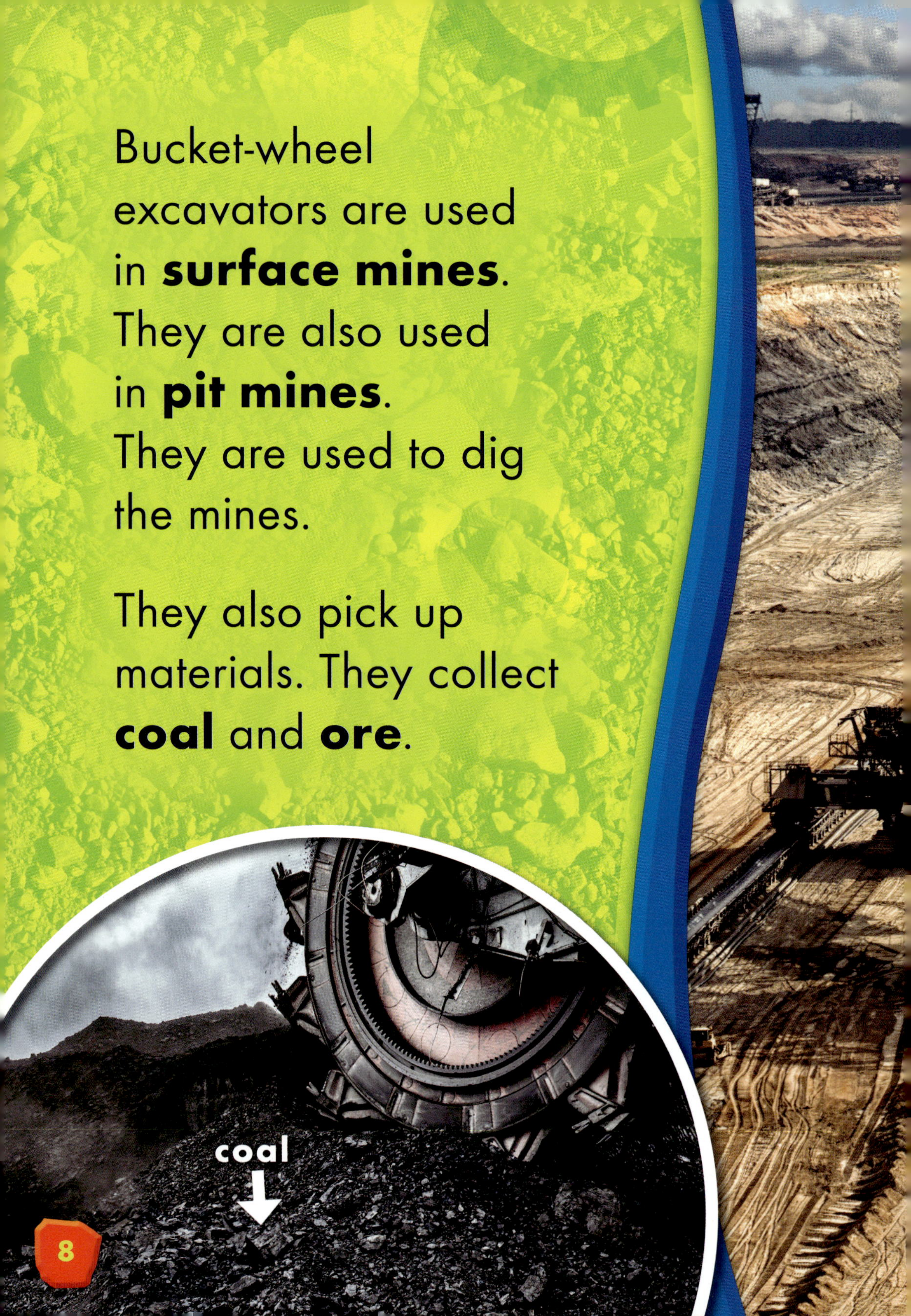

Bucket-wheel excavators are used in **surface mines**. They are also used in **pit mines**. They are used to dig the mines.

They also pick up materials. They collect **coal** and **ore**.

ore
pit mine

Parts of a Bucket-Wheel Excavator

Bucket-wheel excavators have a large wheel. It has buckets all around the outside.

The wheel spins the buckets. The buckets scoop up dirt and ore. They move large amounts in a single day.

The buckets dump their **loads** onto **conveyor belts**. The belts move the dirt the excavator digs up.

Long **booms** help the machines move dirt farther away. The dirt is put into piles.

Bucket-wheel excavators have **tracks**. These help them move from place to place. They travel to different parts of mines.

Bucket-Wheel Excavator Parts

A heavy **counterweight** keeps the machines from tipping over. Strong **supports** help them lift heavy loads.

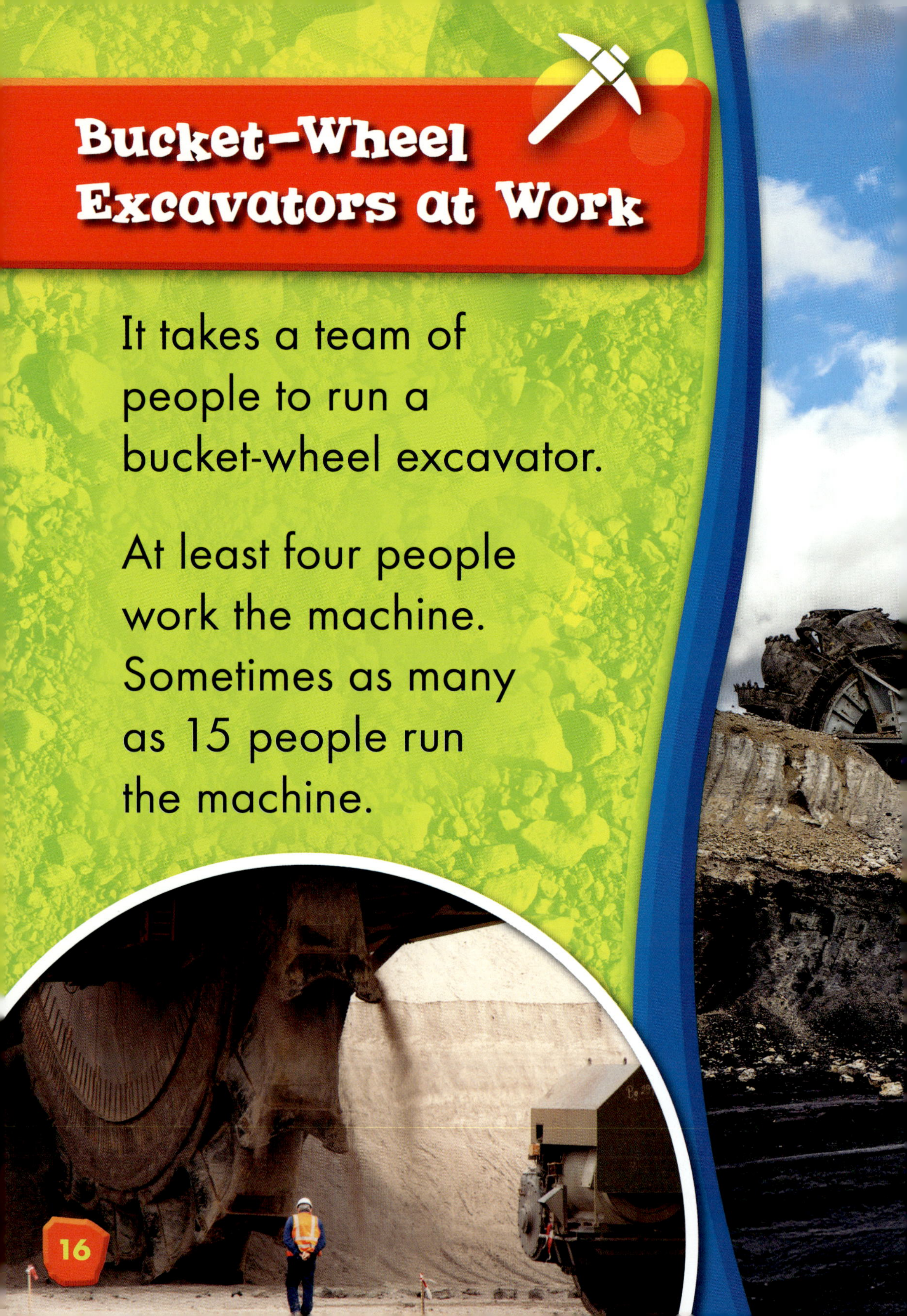

Bucket-Wheel Excavators at Work

It takes a team of people to run a bucket-wheel excavator.

At least four people work the machine. Sometimes as many as 15 people run the machine.

Dirt from the buckets needs to be sorted. The material is separated. Waste is dumped out.

Another conveyor belt moves ore. Dump trucks haul it away.

Bucket-wheel excavators are some of the largest machines in the world. They can dig and move a lot of material.

Bucket-Wheel Excavator Profile

Bagger 293

weighs 15,648 tons (14,196 metric tons)

moves 8.475 million cubic feet (240,000 cubic meters) of dirt each day

moves about 0.4 miles (0.6 kilometers) per hour

takes four years to build one machine

more than 315 feet (96 meters) tall

They help find and move useful material.

Glossary

booms—long arms on excavators

coal—a hard black substance that is burned for fuel

compact—small or close together

conveyor belts—devices that move things from one place to another

counterweight—a heavy object that keeps an excavator balanced

loads—things being carried

material—something that is used to help make something else

ore—a valuable material that occurs naturally in the earth

pit mines—mines that get materials from deep, open holes

supports—beams, wires, and other parts that are used to hold up parts of a machine

surface mines—mines that get materials from near Earth's surface

tracks—moving parts of a machine that touch the ground

To Learn More

AT THE LIBRARY

James, India. *Excavators*. Minneapolis, Minn.: Bellwether Media, 2027.

Rogers, Marie. *Huge Earthmovers*. New York, N.Y.: PowerKids Press, 2022.

Wagner, Zelda. *Bulldozers: A First Look*. Minneapolis, Minn.: Lerner Publications, 2025.

ON THE WEB

FACTSURFER

Factsurfer.com gives you a safe, fun way to find more information.

1. Go to www.factsurfer.com.

2. Enter "bucket-wheel excavators" into the search box and click 🔍.

3. Select your book cover to see a list of related content.

Index

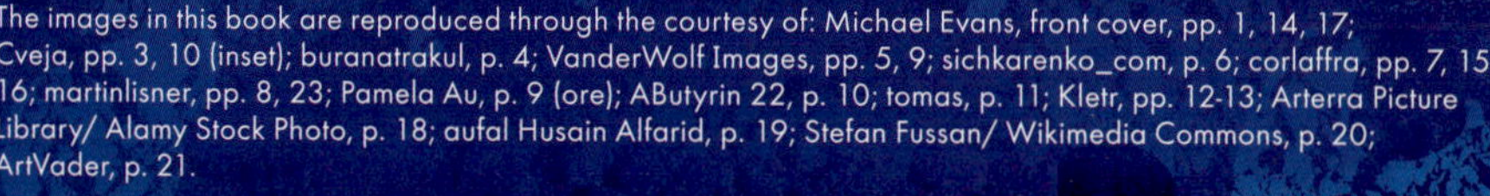

The images in this book are reproduced through the courtesy of: Michael Evans, front cover, pp. 1, 14, 17; Cveja, pp. 3, 10 (inset); buranatrakul, p. 4; VanderWolf Images, pp. 5, 9; sichkarenko_com, p. 6; corlaffra, pp. 7, 15, 16; martinlisner, pp. 8, 23; Pamela Au, p. 9 (ore); AButyrin 22, p. 10; tomas, p. 11; Kletr, pp. 12-13; Arterra Picture Library/ Alamy Stock Photo, p. 18; aufal Husain Alfarid, p. 19; Stefan Fussan/ Wikimedia Commons, p. 20; ArtVader, p. 21.